# LEWISHAM &
# DEPTFORD

## A THIRD SELECTION

### JOHN COULTER

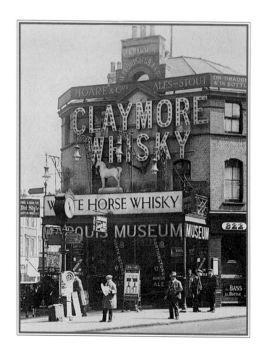

SUTTON PUBLISHING LIMITED

Sutton Publishing Limited
Phoenix Mill · Thrupp · Stroud
Gloucestershire · GL5 2BU

First published 1997

Copyright © John Coulter, 1997

**British Library Cataloguing in Publication Data**
A catalogue record for this book is available from the British Library.

ISBN 0-7509-1462-9

Typeset in 10/12 Perpetua.
Typesetting and origination by
Sutton Publishing Limited.
Printed in Great Britain by
Ebenezer Baylis, Worcester.

# CONTENTS

Lewisham market photographed from a shop at the corner of Romer Avenue (see p. 123) in 1960, when the High Street seemed less troubled with traffic than it is today, after pedestrianisation. To the left of the buses is the old single-storey post office.

# PREFACE

It is sobering to reflect that since I began to compile old photograph books in 1990 I have, either alone or in collaboration, written captions for well over a thousand Lewisham photographs. One might well think this is more than enough, but so far neither the readers nor the material show any sign of exhaustion. Critics might justly feel that the author does. It has been the aim that all of these photos should be different, but with each succeeding volume it becomes more laborious to check this with absolute certainty.

When I began to select pictures for this volume I thought it would probably be necessary to arrange them geographically, with sections devoted to New Cross, Blackheath, Lewisham, etc., but at the layout stage I was pleasantly surprised to find how easily the chosen items fell into the traditional thematic sections. I also feared that it might be hard to maintain the proportion of Deptford photographs at the level of earlier volumes, but in the event the number turned out to be larger than before.

This is the third volume in a series that began with *Lewisham and Deptford in Old Photographs* in 1990, and continued with *Lewisham and Deptford in Old Photographs: a Second Selection* in 1992. Many readers will possess parts one and two, so to avoid wasting valuable space on repetitions I have introduced some cross-references to those volumes. They have been indicated in an abbreviated form. A reference such as 'see I 95' means 'see *Lewisham and Deptford in Old Photographs*, page 95' (I have used the revised second edition of 1992, but this rarely differs substantially from the first). 'See II 15' means 'see *A Second Selection*, page 15'. Cross-references to this present work are given in the simple form 'see p. 107', etc.

One of the most frequent criticisms of my previous volumes has been that they suffer from the lack of an index. Indeed, several kind friends have compiled their own and given me copies, which have proved very useful. Ever ready to listen to advice, Sutton Publishing has now made room for an index in this third volume. Readers will also, I hope, notice a distinct improvement from the greater size and clearer reproduction of the photographs.

# ACKNOWLEDGEMENTS

My thanks to the following for providing photographs, or giving permission for their use: Mrs S. Humphrey, Mr P. Cartwright, Mr R. Cookman, Mr V. Harris, Mr F. Lark, Mr B. Olley, Mr J. Seaman, Mr G. Smith, and the London Borough of Lewisham (Local Studies Centre).

Messrs Ken George, Neil Rhind, John King, and Kenneth Richardson have kindly read through the captions concerned with their specialist fields of knowledge (cinemas, Blackheath, Grove Park, and Grove Park) and made some valuable corrections. The various publications of those gentlemen have been rich quarries for caption material, as in previous volumes. An important new work, published just in time to be of substantial use in this third selection, is *The Streets of London: the Booth Notebooks, South East*, edited by Jess Steele.

# THE RURAL SOUTH

*The approach to Southend Village from the Catford direction on a winter's day nearly a century ago.*

A study in Lewisham High Street – or at least very near it. This photograph was taken by Henry Wood *c.* 1860 in the garden of his father's house, Brooklands. This eighteenth century villa still survives as a shop in the High Street, at the northern corner of Whitburn Road. The grounds of Brooklands ran west to the Ravensbourne and south to Ladywell Road. In this picture Henry Wood captured the view across the river towards the vague outline of Vicar's Hill. It was not until a quarter of a century later that the West Kent Grammar School (now Prendergast's) was built on the summit of Hilly Fields.

An animated scene on old Ladywell Bridge some twenty years before it was widened in 1937–8. The view is westwards towards Brockley. Readers will remember that Ladywell's most famous resident, Henry Williamson, chose *Donkey Boy* as the title for one of his autobiographical novels.

Verdant Lane before the Great War. Hither Green Lane was an extraordinarily long farm track giving access from Lewisham to fields as far away as the modern Downham. Its southern section did not become known as Verdant Lane until the creation of Brownhill Road cut it in half. This postcard was issued before the new name became a joke. The photographer was standing not far from the junction with Whitefoot Lane, and looking north towards Hither Green.

Bellingham Farm (see I 15), probably in the 1920s. The point of view in this photograph was from the lane that connected the farm, via a bridge over the Ravensbourne, with Bromley Road.

Even after building had proceeded some way down it from the Catford end, Bromley Road retained a very rural appearance because of its fine trees and the stream that ran along the east side, crossed at intervals by footbridges for the convenience of the householders. This photograph of *c.* 1910 shows the view south from Inchmery Road.

Bromley Road a little north of Southend Village *c*. 1914. The house on the left was called Ravensbank. It was built *c*. 1900 on the site of the King's Arms public house, which had been demolished as early as 1858. Ivy Cottages, beyond, were used by the Cooper family as a laundry. In the distance are Bellingham Cottages. All these properties were replaced by Dunster House, etc. in the 1950s.

One of the oldest buildings of Grove Park was this cottage, long occupied by labourers of College Farm, Burnt Ash Lane. Until *c*. 1910 it occupied the site nearly opposite Coopers Lane, just north of the spot where Grove Park library now stands. The lady at the gate was possibly Ann Cann, a Norfolk-born widow, who lived here in the 1890s.

A picture that expresses the desolation of progress more eloquently than a thousand words. This was the Ravensbourne at Southend only a lifetime ago.

The house and forge of Frederick James Harris, the Southend Village shoeing smith, stood near the corner of Whitefoot Lane, nearly opposite the Tiger's Head. They were shortly to be demolished, together with the unhappily named New Cottages on the right, when this photograph was taken *c.* 1912. In 1914 Harris moved across the road to part of the redundant Lower Mill.

Southend House, the largest mansion in the village, was demolished in the 1830s and its grounds used to enlarge the garden of Southend Hall. The Forsters retained some of the outbuildings as their home farm. They included this cottage, seen here *c.* 1860, which stood in Bromley Road, nearly opposite the Upper Mill, until *c.* 1900. Nos. 391 to 397 are now on its site.

The Upper Mill at Southend Village (see II 44) came to be known as Perry's Mill in the late nineteenth century, after the family who were the last millers, and the tenants for many years. Jacob Perry, a prominent local personality, in fact turned his attention more and more to farming and the sale of timber.

Perry Hill is one of the oldest inhabited parts of Lewisham, so it is rather startling to find that as late as 1910 it could still present such a rural aspect to the photographer. This is the bend where Selworthy Road now meets Perry Hill, seen from the Bell Green direction. It was not intensively developed until the grounds of the Manor House, on the left, and Clare Lodge, on the right, became available *c.* 1930.

Rose Cottage in Mill Gardens, Sydenham. This little group of weather-boarded houses was built in the 1820s or '30s on the newly enclosed Sydenham Common. The road was named after the windmill that stood here until the 1880s. Rose Cottage was demolished a year or two after this photograph was taken in 1960.

# THE INDUSTRIAL NORTH

*The mast pond and sheds at the Royal Victoria Victualling Yard. (See II 50.)*

Two years after its closure in 1869 the Royal Dockyard at Deptford was re-opened by the Corporation of London as a depot for the import and slaughtering of live meat. The Foreign Cattle Market continued to operate until 1913. This is the main gate in Prince Street *c.* 1900. The site is now Convoys Wharf, a centre for the import of paper for what used to be called Fleet Street.

The great engineering firm of John Penn & Sons had its boiler works on the Thames at Deptford (see I 107), and the engine works, seen here *c.* 1862, in Blackheath Road. There was constant movement of machinery between the two, by horse-drawn carts during the day, and by traction engines at night.

The derelict Lewisham Silk Mills seen from the main gate, at the junction of Morden Hill and Conington Road, in 1937, shortly before demolition. From the fourteenth century this had been the Armoury Mill, used to grind steel for the Royal Armoury. Later it produced swords and muskets. From *c.* 1820 the mill was converted to the processing of silk, and the production of gold and silver thread for uniforms, etc. The business was killed by khaki.

A scene on Deptford Creek in the late 1940s, when the Ravensbourne was still a busy working river. The grain barges were lying off Robinson's flour mill, just north of Deptford Bridge.

The dynamic John Lane Densham took hold of his family's old-fashioned business and transformed it into the mighty Mazawattee Tea Company by his introduction of Ceylon packet tea. He then diversified into cocoa, chocolate, and coffee, and in 1901 built a huge factory (seen above when just completed) at New Cross, on the Surrey Canal. What little survives of the building is now part of the Elizabeth Industrial Estate, north of New Cross Gate station.

C.H. Musselwhite Ltd. established themselves on the Surrey Canal as whiting and distemper manufacturers c. 1870, and remained in business for nearly a century. The photograph shows their factory in the 1940s, as seen from the Deptford Wharf railway lift bridge (see p. 95). The area has changed completely, and 1 to 43 Carteret Way now stand on the site of the whiting works.

Thomas Letts, the diary publisher, lived at Clare Lodge, Perry Hill (see p. 14). In the mid 1860s he built a large factory called the General Printing Office in North Road, the present Goodwood Road, next to what is now New Cross Gate station. The building later became the works of the Aspinall Enamel Co., and was not surprisingly gutted by fire (above), probably in the late 1890s. This was not the end of the story, for the factory was rebuilt with little external alteration, and survived until the 1960s as Halstead's distemper works. It is seen below in 1939.

Deptford Creek seen from the Greenwich side of Creek Bridge in the late 1940s. The Thames is just out of sight around the bend of the river. The words on the building above the boat are 'The General Steam Navigation Co.'

Job Heath, who learnt his trade in the brickfields of his native Norwood, moved to College Farm, Brockley in the 1880s. Here he founded the Crofton Park brickworks, and his firm went on to build much of Ladywell. The photograph shows some of his employees in the 1890s. (See p. 38 and I 103.)

As part of its effort to relieve unemployment during the Depression the London County Council decided in 1931 to build a storm water discharge culvert from its Deptford pumping station on the Creek. The contract was awarded to Kinnear, Mordie, & Co. of Hither Green Lane, who found work for 165 men. Some of them are seen above in the tunnel, and the completed culvert is shown below.

Folkestone Gardens, seven large blocks of 'working class dwellings', were built between Trundleys Road and the London and Greenwich Railway in 1897–8. The architects were Humphreys, Davies, and Co. and H.S. Saunders, sizeable forces for so dismal a result. Two of the blocks were destroyed by a V2 rocket on 7 March 1945, with the loss of fifty-two lives. This view of the largest of all the blocks was taken *c.* 1970, a couple of years before the remaining five were demolished, and replaced by the park called Folkestone Gardens.

Despite its poverty and industrialisation Deptford returned Conservatives to parliament until 1906, when the first Labour member was elected. He was the Right Hon. Charles William Bowerman (1851–1947), who also had the distinction of being the longest-serving Deptford MP. He retained the seat until 1931. Bowerman was a leading trade unionist, who served as President, and later as Secretary, of the TUC.

# VANISHING HOUSES

*The Chestnuts, 13 Dorville Road, Lee, was one of a group of six matching houses built in the late 1870s, and demolished c. 1974. Millmark Way now occupies the site.*

Crossfield Lane began as a useful short cut for travellers from London to Greenwich. By the early eighteenth century the south side was lined with small houses, all now demolished. Among the last to go were nos. 12, 10 (with the archway) and 8, seen here in the 1960s. Deptford High Street is in the background.

William Street, a development of the mid 1860s, originally linked Staunton Street to Abinger Road, but in 1899 it was made part of Staunton Street. This house, the most easterly on the north side, then became no. 26. It was bombed in the Second World War, and the rest of the road followed it into oblivion soon afterwards. The garages between Wardalls House and the Evelyn Hall have replaced no. 26.

58 St. Donatt's Road, Brockley, a house of the early 1860s, is seen here in 1912, when William Brown was the tenant. Nos. 46 to 62 were destroyed during the Blitz, and the flats known as Hawthorn House have taken their place.

Wickham Terrace in Lewisham Way was built between 1849 and 1855. The twenty-five houses, split into three groups by Manor Avenue and Wickham Road, formed the public frontage of the ambitious Wickham-Drake estate. The fine composition has been ruined during and since the Second World War, but the houses seen here *c.* 1900 (nos. 178 to 160) do survive. In the distance is Brockley Congregational Church, at the corner of Upper Brockley Road. It was demolished in 1968.

Two of the most prominent Blackheath buildings are Mill House and Golf House, which stand to the north-west of Blackheath Vale. They were built in 1836, on the site of the windmill known as the West Mill. This photograph, probably taken before 1914, shows Mill House, the north-eastern half of the pair.

Wemyss Cottage was probably built by John Sheepshanks, a noted patron of British artists, in the early 1830s, on the site of an existing house. The gardens stretched down to Pond Road, of which the house was a part before Wemyss Road was built. This 1913 view from Pond Road shows how apt was the original name of the property, Fairlawn.

Isleham, 17 The Glebe, Lee, *c.* 1910. The man with the bicycle was Morriss William Brown, the owner. The house was built *c.* 1850, and destroyed by a bomb during the Second World War. (See II 118 and 120.)

These houses, 1–4 The Orchard, Blackheath, were built *c.* 1897, and are seen here about ten years later. The site had been part of the garden of the large eighteenth century mansion of the same name (see II 104), which soon came to be known as 5 The Orchard. It stood back from the new houses, in the gap seen on the left of this picture.

Belmont Lodge, later known as St. Lawrence, was numbered 2 Brandram Road even though its main entrance (as seen in this 1961 photograph) was in Blessington Road. It was built *c.* 1860, and survived until the early 1960s. Nos. 2, 2A, and 2B, and the Ranyard Memorial Nursing Home, have replaced it.

Ravensbourne Terrace, which consisted of seven or more houses (as the sub-division varied), was built *c.* 1810 in the part of Morden Hill that lies south of Lewisham Road. The original occupants were probably workers at the Armoury Mill (see p. 17). This photograph shows part of the terrace in 1937, seven years before it was wrecked by a flying bomb. (See II 107, where the date should be corrected.)

The Hollebones of Ravensbourne Park House (see II 100) left Catford a year or so after the death of old Mrs Hollebone in the summer of 1890. These photographs, taken in 1891, were intended as a memento of the thirty years the family had spent in the house. In the top picture the man on the front steps was probably the eldest son Frederick Hollebone, who ran the family wine business, and in the gig is most likely his brother Charles, a stockbroker. The bottom picture shows two of the servants by the back door.

This seventeenth century weather-boarded house in Sydenham Road was occupied from 1860 until his death in 1900 by Sir George Grove, the Secretary of the Crystal Palace, and the founder of the great musical dictionary. The house was demolished in 1929. There is a plaque in honour of Sir George on the wall of the Catholic presbytery, which now occupies the site.

Orielton, no. 45, and Fairmount Lodge, no. 47 Brockley View, seen *c.* 1970, some five years before both were pulled down. The open space on the left is part of Blythe Hill Fields. The two houses were built in the optimistic early days of the Brockley Park estate, Fairmount Lodge in the 1870s, Orielton in the 1880s. Nos. 31 to 45 now stand on their site.

# ON THE STREETS

*The Obelisk junction, where Lewisham High Street meets Loampit Vale, has been almost totally transformed since this postcard was issued c. 1910.*

The northern end of Tanners Hill in 1896, when these eighteenth century houses were awaiting demolition so that the Broadway Theatre (see I 122) could replace them. New Cross Road is in the distance. Annie Day, the wife of James Day, had her dressmaking and millinery business at no. 18, and Ann Hopkins had the old clothes shop at no. 16. On the left is part of no. 20 (see p. 75).

Union Street, Deptford, which was later part of Creek Road, and is now known as Albury Street, was named after the parliamentary union with Scotland of 1707. Many of the houses were built by Thomas Lucas, the master bricklayer employed on St. Paul's church. They were very smart in the eighteenth century, but by the 1920s, when this photograph was probably taken, they had been broken up into squalid flats or single rooms. (See also I 28.)

Two Edwardian postcards of Deptford High Street. The one above, taken from the Broadway or New Cross Road end, makes an interesting comparison with the picture at I 29. The photograph below looks southwards towards the railway bridge from the gates of St. Paul's Church, and features two public houses. On the right is the Windsor Castle (empty and boarded-up for several years) at the corner of Ffinch Street, and on the left the Royal Oak (no longer a pub) at the corner of Crossfield Lane.

The north side of Giffin Street (nos. 5, 7, 9, etc.) seen from the Deptford High Street end in the 1940s. Thomas Giffin, a Southwark builder, was a busy developer in Deptford during the 1770s. He was involved in the creation of Effingham Street (later Effingham Place, and now Frankham Street) as well as being the chief promoter of Giffin Street in 1775–6. Like so many speculative builders he soon over-reached himself, and was declared a bankrupt in 1779, but his name lives on. The same cannot be said for his houses. All of these were demolished in 1955–6.

Hamilton Street, a development of the 1840s, is seen here a hundred years later. This view of the north side looks towards Deptford High Street. The taller building breaking the line of the terrace was the Railway Tavern, which stood at the corner of Grinling Place. The pub and the houses (except no. 56, nearest to the High Street) were demolished in the 1960s.

The Blackhorse Bridge, which carried Evelyn Street over the Surrey Canal, was a narrow structure until 1888. In that year the Greenwich Board of Works, then the local authority for Deptford, rebuilt the bridge to make it suitable for the new horse trams. This photograph, looking towards London, with the gasholder on the right, was taken soon afterwards.

Baildon Street, a cul-de-sac to the north of New Cross Road, was built in the early 1850s, and was originally known as Moore Street. It was 'nicknamed Tug-of-War Street because so many fights take place here'. By 1901, when this prize collection of urchins gathered for a photographer, it had become one of the worst slums in Deptford. 'If any men and women have the criminal brand on their faces,' an observer noted in 1899, 'these seem unmistakenly to bear it.' Baildon Street still exists as a name, but is now just a service road between blocks of flats.

This photograph of *c*. 1910 shows a part of Queens Road, New Cross (between Pomeroy Street and Kender Street) from which all the old houses have been swept away. The view is eastwards towards New Cross Gate. The premises of Horatio Kemp, the auctioneer, estate agent, bailiff, undertaker, etc. were at 179 Queens Road.

Kitto Road seen from opposite the Duke of Albany, *c.* 1910. On the left are Bousfield Road and the Methodist Church, which was built in 1898, and destroyed by a rocket in 1945. It was rebuilt in 1958, but is now the Church of the God of Prophecy. At no. 41, just past the church, the novelist Joyce Cary lived with his family from 1897 to 1900. This house, blue plaque material, was another victim of the rocket.

This busy scene in Lewisham High Road, now Lewisham Way, was captured outside Goldsmiths' College *c.* 1910. The road has survived better than many in Lewisham, and the majority of these 1850s houses are still standing. One loss is Brockley Congregational Church, the spire of which can be seen in the distance.

The view north along Howson Road from the corner of Whitbread Road, *c.* 1914. The houses on the right, nos. 95 to 85, have now been removed for the enlargement of the St. Mary Magdalen School. Howson Road was long the home of David Jones, one of Lewisham's most distinguished residents. Those familiar with his paintings will recognise the atmosphere.

A new and unmade Phoebeth Road *c.* 1905, showing the view north to Ladywell Road. The streets on this estate were named after the children of the Heath family, the builders, who were too numerous to christen one each. Walter Francis Heath had his home and yard at no. 9, the gates of which are just out of sight on the right of this picture. (See p. 20.)

Lewisham Bridge *c*. 1914. The Duke of Cambridge pub and St. Stephen's Church are in the background. On the left is a rare glimpse of the Obelisk Cinema, a flea-pit that only lasted from 1912 until 1923. The turning to the right of the picture, Mill Road, has also ceased to exist.

When William Perkins, or his partner Mr Venimore, climbed to the roof of the London & Provincial Bank (now Barclays) to take this photograph, *c*. 1900, he saw the big shops of Stroud and Chiesman on the right, and the Salisbury, Roebuck, and Duke of Cambridge pubs on the left. If he could return today he would be startled by the disappearance not only of nearly all the buildings, but even of the clock tower, the recent move of which has taken it out of the line of this shot.

An excellent bustling view of the centre of Lewisham *c.* 1910, with the spire of the Methodist church (see p. 56) overlooking the scene from Albion Way. The clock tower was already looking weatherbeaten, little more than a decade after it was built. Behind it was the London and Provincial Bank (now Barclays), the only surviving building in the picture. The two groups of low shops to the right of the bank were relics from the original development of the island site between the High Street and Lewis Grove in the years around 1820. The post office has now replaced several of the old cottages in the nearer group. The large building with the parapet, to the right of the picture, was the Albion pub. Like so much else in this part of the High Street it was destroyed by the flying bomb of the 28 July 1944. (See I 156.)

Two complementary views of the Lewisham High Street, Belmont Hill, Lee High Road, and Lewis Grove junction, *c.* 1930. The picture above, taken from Belmont Hill, shows E.A. Dubois's department store and the Midland Bank on the two corners of Lewis Grove, and the back of the White Horse on the left. The picture below, taken from Lewis Grove, shows the White Horse again on the right. On the left are nos. 11 to 29 Belmont Hill, ten houses that were destroyed during the Second World War. They had been built between 1839 and 1841, and were originally known as Belmont Place.

In the 1860s and '70s Eastdown Park, now just a road, was the name for a smart new middle-class district of Lewisham, which also included Wisteria Road, Dermody Road and part of Gilmore Road. This Edwardian postcard shows the southern end of Wisteria Road (see II 145) from Dermody Road. These houses were built in the late 1870s and most of them are still standing. Those on the right, nos. 49, 47, etc., were known originally as Lansdowne Terrace. On the left are the old Cambridge Villas (nos. 68, 66, etc.). Here only the houses in the picture have survived. Nos. 54 to 60 were destroyed by bombing, and have been rebuilt. The lower numbered houses beyond have been replaced more recently by the developments known as Wright Close and Trinity Close.

The view north up Dacre Park, *c.* 1919. Most of these 1840s houses are still standing, and are now numbered 75 to 97. Only the most distant block, beyond Eton Grove, has been demolished. The four pairs with debased pediments were originally known as Kingswood Terrace.

This view up Lee Road was taken from a little north of Manor Way, *c.* 1912. It shows on the left nos. 52, 50, and 48 Lee Road, houses built *c.* 1862–3 and demolished almost exactly a century later. Nos. 62 to 72 are now on their site. The old no. 52, The Rowans, was the home of General Robert Shortrede, mathematician and astronomer, in the 1860s.

The view west along Lee High Road from Manor Park probably just before 1914. On the left are the Rose of Lee, as rebuilt *c.* 1897, and the Lee Baptist Chapel, which was destroyed by a bomb in the Second World War. On the right is Manor Park Parade, a terrace of shops built in 1895. In 1899 it was noted that it enjoyed only 'moderate trade', and that the shopkeepers 'change frequently'.

Lee Park was an old footpath, providing a useful shortcut from the village of Lee to Blackheath. It did not attract the attention of building developers until the 1840s. The feature that sets it apart is the remarkable avenue of trees standing not on the pavement but in the road itself. Lee Park is seen here from the Blackheath end in 1905. The number of trees is sadly diminished today.

Farley Road in the 1920s, showing the view westwards towards the older detached houses at the Rushey Green end. The large, distant shape on the right is the back of the New Embassy Billiard Hall (now a shop) at 75 Rushey Green. It opened *c.* 1923.

Ravensbourne Park, long one of Lewisham's most fashionable roads, is seen here *c.* 1914. The houses shown are between Bourneville Road and Westdown Road. Nos. 52 and 50, on the left, at the corner of Bourneville Road, were built *c.* 1906, and nos. 48 to 42 *c.* 1870. All still survive.

Brownhill Road seen from the corner of Laleham Road *c.* 1906, with the Baptist Church on the crest of the hill in the distance. The gap between the terraces on the right was plugged in 1907, when Norfolk and Prior of Catford Road built nos. 134 to 170 Brownhill Road.

The buildings shown in this Edwardian study of Catford Hill are unchanged, but the atmosphere is rather different today. The photographer was standing at the corner of River View Park and looking north towards Catford Bridge. The houses on the left (nos. 106, 104, etc., at the corner of Beechfield Road) were built *c.* 1895 on the site of the villa called Catford House.

Shortly before the Great War Samuel Phillips, the prolific Catford photographer, could safely set up his tripod in the middle of Perry Hill, outside the Rutland Tavern, to capture this lively scene. The shops on the right, now nos. 51, 49, etc., were built in the late 1870s, and originally called The Pavement.

Perry Vale c. 1910, at its junction with Sunderland Road. These houses, nos. 153 (at the corner) to 131, were built c. 1903 by Edward Christmas of Dartmouth Road. The initial letters of the names he gave to the houses spelt out 'Ted Christmas', but several have now sadly been altered or removed.

This view down Tyson Road from Honor Oak Road has not changed too much because these houses on the north side (built in the late 1870s) have mostly survived. The equally impressive group on the south side, built a few years earlier, has, on the other hand, been totally destroyed.

And all is dullest suburbia . . . This is Baring Road, looking north towards the station, *c.* 1930. The houses on the left were the eastern ramparts of the great Downham Estate, built by the London County Council in the 1920s. Photographs taken only fifteen years earlier show this as an idyllically beautiful country lane.

# CHURCHES GOING
# & GONE

*St. Mary's, Lewisham High Street, c. 1870, before the proportions of George Gibson's 1770s church were ruined by Sir Arthur Blomfield's heavy chancel. (See p. 55.)*

St. Luke's Church in Evelyn Street was built in 1870–72. The architect was T.H. Watson. This 1901 photograph shows the interior, which has now been greatly altered.

The parish of St. Mark, Deptford, had a brief existence. The church in Edward Street (seen here in 1918) was opened in 1883, but in 1950 the parish was re-united with St. Paul's. The building lives on, though, despite serious bomb damage in 1942, and the demolition of all its neighbouring houses in the 1970s. The St. Mark's Institute, as it is called now, stands isolated in the middle of New Deptford Green.

The Deptford Central Hall band *c*. 1906. It was a victim of the Great War. In 1917 the minister noted sadly that 'our Silver Band has lost its conductor and most of its members and is only a shadow of its former self'. The Central Hall in Creek Road was the headquarters of the Deptford Methodist Mission. It was built in 1903, seriously damaged by bombing in 1940, and rebuilt in 1956.

The New Cross Wesleyan Church, New Cross Road, was built in 1872, nearly opposite the Marquis of Granby. The impressive interior is seen here *c*. 1905. The church was destroyed by a flying bomb in 1944, and the congregation disbanded in the next year. The site lay vacant for decades, but the inevitable Goldsmiths' College has recently used the ground to build Dean House. (See p. 102.)

The Brockley Baptist Church (seen here *c.* 1904). It was built in what is now Upper Brockley Road in 1867. It was badly damaged during the Blitz, but has survived. The contemporary houses in the foreground, nos. 72 to 62, are also happily still standing.

The St. Mary Magdelen Roman Catholic Church in Howson Road, Brockley was built in 1899. It was damaged in 1940, but has been restored. Father Louis Deydier was the priest in charge before and during the Great War.

The Honor Oak Park Wesleyan Church in Brockley Rise was built in 1888. This photograph shows it about ten years later. The church was destroyed by a flying bomb in 1944, but the congregation continued to meet for a time in the schoolroom, around the corner in Ackroyd Road. This is now the Ackroyd Community Centre. The houses numbered 2 to 12 Ackroyd Road stand on the site of the church.

St. Cyprian's Church originated in a mission hall in Brockley Road, which still survives as the Brockley Catholic Social Club. The church itself was built in Adelaide Road (now Avenue) in 1901. This postcard shows it soon afterwards. The church was destroyed in 1940, and the site is now covered by auxiliary buildings for Prendergast's School.

Most of the Anglican churches built to relieve pressure on St. Margaret's, Lee were damaged or destroyed in the Second World War. This photograph of *c.* 1870 shows Holy Trinity Church, Glenton Road, which was built in 1863 by Lewis Glenton, the developer responsible for the surrounding houses. The church was smashed in 1944, and its parish re-absorbed by St. Margaret's four years later.

The Bromley Road Tabernacle, later known as the South Lee Baptist Church, and now the South Lee Christian Centre, was founded in the early 1870s. This iron church at the corner of Baring Road (formerly Bromley Road) and Waite Davies Road (formerly Butterfield Street) was built in 1896. It was replaced by the present church (see I 69) in 1911.

The east end of St. Mary's Church (see p. 49) before and after the unfortunate remodelling carried out by Sir Arthur Blomfield in 1881–2. His new chancel involved the removal of the most notable monuments to less appropriate positions. Flaxman's fine memorial to Mary Lushington, seen below the gallery on the right in the top photograph, is now to be found on the north wall. E.H. Bailey's huge monument to John Thackeray was moved to the west end of the church.

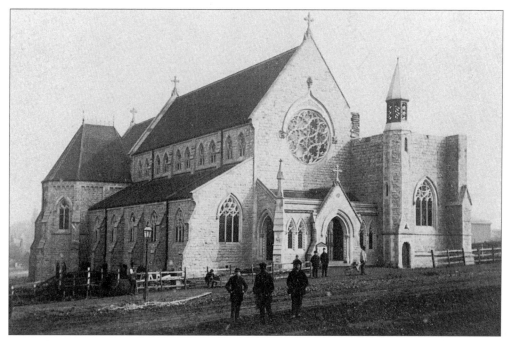

The College Park estate at Lewisham was built over the fields of College Farm in the 1860s and '70s. Its parish church was St. Mark's, seen here in 1870, when just completed. The photographer was standing in the area now occupied by Bonfield Road. Between him and the church ran a tentative Clarendon Road (now Rise). St. Mark's was declared redundant in 1960, and demolished in 1968–9.

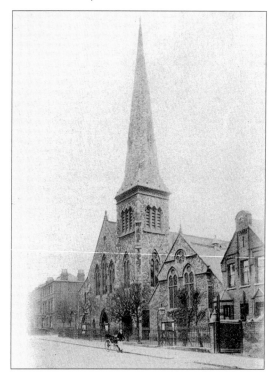

A near neighbour to St. Mark's was the Lewisham Methodist Church in Albion Road (now Albion Way). The photograph shows it *c.* 1905. It was built in 1870, and destroyed in the Blitz. The church has just been rebuilt for the second time since the war. In confirmation of the new focus of human worship, the car park is now bigger than the church.

The Lewisham Unitarian Church was built in the garden of Sion House, next door to the old library, in 1910. It was severely damaged during the Second World War, but restored in 1952. This photograph shows a special Christmas Day service for the lonely in 1961. In 1967 the building was purchased by the library service as a bindery and acquisitions centre. It was demolished in 1994. The Unitarians now meet in Bromley Road.

St. Saviour's Roman Catholic Church in Lewisham High Street was built in 1909. This photograph was taken in 1929, when the presbytery was built next door, and the church was embellished with its most distinctive feature, the tall campanile.

An altogether less showy Catholic church is Holy Cross, Sangley Road, which was built in 1903–4, and enlarged in 1924. It was damaged in the Blitz, and has twice been struck by lightning, but survives little altered from its appearance when this photograph was taken *c.* 1905.

The first Trinity Congregational Church was built in Ravensbourne Park, Catford, in 1857, through the enthusiastic efforts of the Rev. Thomas Timpson, the minister of the Union Chapel at Lewisham. In 1867 the Trinity Church moved to the corner of Stanstead Road and Faversham Road. The second church is seen here *c.* 1910. It was rebuilt on a much smaller scale in the 1960s.

The Hither Green Wesleyan Church, designed by the firm of Gordon, Lowther, and Gunton in 1900, stood on a prominent site at the junction of Hither Green Lane and Wellmeadow Road. Its destruction in 1940 was a sad loss to a district crying out for architectural variety. This postcard shows the range of halls and schools that stood behind the church in Hither Green Lane.

St. George's, Perry Hill, which stands in fact in the angle of Woolstone and Vancouver Roads, was designed by W.C. Banks of Lewisham, and built between 1878 and 1880. It was looking very well when this photograph was taken *c.* 1905, but is now a sad sight, struggling for survival under the threat of subsidence.

St. John the Baptist, Bromley Road, seen from Whitefoot Lane in the late 1920s. The church, designed by Sir Charles Nicholson, was completed (as far as it ever was completed) in 1928. The surprise about St. John's is that it contains some fine memorials of the Forster family, the earlier ones removed there from the old chapel next door.

The concentration of a large German population in Sydenham and Forest Hill, perhaps attracted by the fame and musical life of the Crystal Palace, led to the building of the German Evangelical Church in Dacres Road in 1883. The original church, seen here *c.* 1905, was destroyed by bombing in 1944, but a replacement was built in 1958–9. Dietrich Bonhoeffer was pastor in the 1930s, and the new church is named in his honour.

# HAPPIEST DAYS?

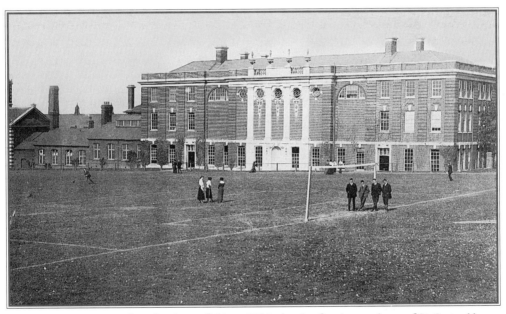

*Goldsmiths' College from the playing fields c. 1908, shortly after the completion of Sir Reginald Blomfield's new wing, which dominates the picture.*

Two scenes of Edwardian student life at Goldsmiths' College. The group above, possibly during a rag week, was gathered at the pavilion, which used to stand at the south-western corner of the college, behind the garden of 26 St. Donatt's Road. The swimming pool, which had been added in the 1890s, suffered the unlikely fate of being destroyed by fire in 1945. (See I 78, 99, and 100.)

Belmont House School, 40 Lee Terrace, was a boarding establishment for boys, run, when this photograph was taken *c.* 1905, by the Rev. Percy Urwick Lasbery. The house, which had been built *c.* 1834, still survives, but has been sadly altered to fit it for its new role as part of the Blackheath Hospital.

Ashby College was a boarding school for girls that occupied nos. 40 and 42 Wickham Road, Brockley, *c.* 1895 to 1905. This card, although captioned 'Ashby College', confusingly only shows part of the school: no. 40 is the house on the left, but the other is no. 38. These fine houses, built in 1876, are still standing.

The Claremont House School for Ladies at 334 Brownhill Road at the time when it was conducted by Miss Bishop, between 1903 and 1913. It had been built *c.* 1897, as one of the largest style of house on the Corbett Estate, and was originally known as 21 Queen's Gardens. The conservatory has been lost, but otherwise the house survives with little alteration.

Nos. 22 and 23 Montpelier Row, houses built *c.* 1797, were usually occupied as a single unit from 1860 until 1959. When this photograph was taken the building (seen on the left) housed St. Christopher's College for Training Sunday School Teachers. This institution, founded in 1908, proved an unlikely success, and in 1916 it had to move to the larger Westcombe House, in Vanbrugh Park.

Middle-class schools sprang up after 1870 for the convenience of parents who could not afford public schools, but who did not want their daughters to mix with the *hoi polloi* at the church or Board school. The St. Margaret's Higher Grade School in Old Road, Lee (see I 94) fell into this category. The top picture shows the rear of the building *c.* 1910. Below are the junior girls in 1915. Mrs Townsend, the head mistress, is on the right.

The Haberdashers' Aske's Hatcham Boys' School, the very name of which should give its pupils an excellent grounding in grammar, was designed by William Snooke, surveyor to the Company, and built in 1875. It originally housed the boys' and girls' schools, but the boys inherited the whole building when the girls moved down the hill in 1891. The 1836 statue of Robert Aske, the seventeenth century founder of the charity, was transferred from the old almshouses and school at Hoxton. It was the work of Coggan & Co., the successors to the famous Mrs Coade. In the picture below some Edwardian Askeans are seen at work in 'the physical laboratory'.

St. Dunstan's College (see I 91) was opened in 1888, and almost immediately established a formidable reputation. This aerial view was taken *c.* 1924, when the houses curving round from Ravensbourne Park into Ravensbourne Park Crescent (top left) were being built. Faversham Road is in the foreground. What looks like a railway (bottom right) is Stanstead Road complete with tram lines.

The playground of Prendergast's School (formally the Lewisham Grammar School for Girls) in the 1920s. It opened here in Rushey Green in 1890, and remained for 105 years before moving to its splendid new home on Hilly Fields. The old building has now been demolished, and its site is set aside for a health centre.

The staff of the Hedgley Street Infants' School, Lee, in 1892. They were Miss Brissenden, the head mistress, in the centre, her deputy Miss Bearman, probably on the right, the three pupil teachers Lily Ford, Henrietta Simmonds, and Rosalie Dixon, and in the foreground, the monitor Rose Dawtry. She was about to escape, through marriage, from the academic grind. The Hedgley Street National Schools, which were founded and financed by the Church of England, eventually developed into the present Northbrook School.

These two photographs of Sandhurst Road school, Catford, (the lower one showing the boys at 'drill') were taken in 1904, immediately after the doors opened. The exterior view was taken from Ardgowan Road. The school was designed by Thomas J. Bailey, architect to the London School Board, but the project moved so slowly that by the time the work was finished the Board had been abolished, and the job had to be completed by the London County Council. Only part of Bailey's building, one of his finest, survived the notorious bombing raid of 1943, in which so many children and teachers were killed.

The site for Ennersdale School was acquired in the 1880s, but jealous opposition from the headmaster of Hither Green School in Beacon Road meant that a temporary iron structure was not erected until 1895, and the present building only in 1897–8. It cost £21,000, and provided places for 800 children. This class of infants was photographed *c.* 1911.

Monson Road School (see I 97) had its origin in classes held at the All Saints' Institute. They met there until the School Board for London provided this grim building in 1882. It was known as Cold Blow Lane School before the name was changed to Monson Road. The odd thing is that its principal front, seen here, faces Hunsdon Road.

Mantle Road School at Brockley put on a mammoth entertainment for Christmas 1913, which, in addition to excerpts from *She Stoops to Conquer* and various 'vocal items', included two complete plays. This was the cast of *In the Days of King Charles*, with words and music by members of the staff.

The St. John's National Schools were built in what was then St. John's Road, now Albyn Road, in 1855. They were rebuilt by the LCC as The Ravensbourne School in 1910, and have since had many names. Recently they have returned to their Anglican roots as St. Stephen's School. This was the school house in Seymour Street in 1911, the year of its demolition. Outside were Maude and Violet Cartwright, the wife and daughter of the caretaker, Robert.

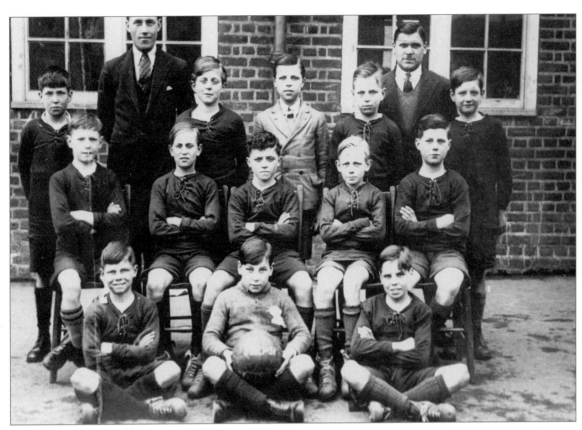

When the great Bellingham and Downham housing estates were built by the London County Council between 1919 and 1930, a tremendous burden was thrown upon the ingenuity of the street-naming department. As work on the Downham estate reached a climax it was decided (probably by a County Hall official unable to distinguish between King Alfred and King Arthur) to call a number of the new roads after the knights of the round table and their adventures. Hence Gareth, Launcelot, Galahad, Bedivere Roads, etc. Pendragon Road was the chosen site for one of the estate's original primary schools. It opened in the 1920s, while building work continued all around. This was the fearsome looking football team in the 1930/31 season. No doubt they were the terror of the Lewisham junior league, as schools from council estates have usually tended to be. Pendragon still exists, now as one of the borough's special schools.

# IN THE PUBLIC SERVICE

*The Figure Room at the Horniman Museum, Forest Hill, not long after it was completed in 1901. (See I 124 and II 71.)*

The influence of the London County Council on the borough was generally destructive, but it did provide Deptford with these two striking fire stations. The one in Evelyn Street (above) was built in 1903. The walls to the left of the picture are those of St. Luke's Church (see p. 50). The New Cross fire station in Queen's Road (below) was built in 1894 (see II 137). The 1850s and '60s terraces opposite were swept away in the 1960s by that same LCC.

This building at 20 Tanners Hill has had a varied career. It began as the St. Paul's Vestry Offices, served from 1900 to 1905 as Deptford's first town hall, and has since been a social club, cinema, sweet factory, Liberal HQ, and warehouse. When this photograph was taken in the 1920s it was the Deptford New Town Social Club. (See I 114.)

The inadequate 20 Tanners Hill was replaced in 1905 by a Deptford Town Hall that was widely considered as outrageously extravagant. Now we are free simply to admire the work of Lancaster, Stewart, & Rickards. They were the winners of an architectural competition in which the other contestants (who included Sir Alfred Brunwell Thomas of Deptford library and the Addey and Stanhope school) contributed dull, conventional Edwardian municipal designs. For once the judges got it right. (See I 114 and 155, and II 134.)

The New Cross public baths in Laurie Grove were built between 1895 and 1898 to the designs of Thomas Dinwiddy, another unsuccessful competitor in the town hall competition a few years later. This must have been a blow to him, as the two buildings had been conceived very much as a group. The baths closed in 1991 and like the town hall have been taken over by Goldsmiths' College, which is rapidly monopolising New Cross.

Councillor Berryman, the Mayor of Deptford, laying the foundation stone of the old New Cross library on the 6 September 1910. It was opened ten months later. The architects, possibly the two men to the right of the mace bearer, were Sydney Castle and Gerald Warren. Either they or the builder, F.J. Gorham, must have been incompetent, for in 1928 the library had to be practically rebuilt because of 'structural deterioration'.

The present Hatcham Liberal Club in Queen's Road has the inscription 'founded 1880', but that does not refer to the existing building, which dates only from about 1911. The club's two previous homes (though not its earliest if '1880' is correct) were in New Cross Road, at the surviving no. 124, in 1884–5, and afterwards at Portland House, seen here posing for a Christmas card in the early years of the twentieth century. There was a house on this site from at least as early as the 1720s. From the 1750s it was the first headquarters of the Edmonds family, who became one of the leading New Cross market gardening dynasties. Robert Edmonds probably rebuilt Portland House in the form seen here in 1804. It was later occupied by one of the branches of the Hardcastle family of Hatcham House, and in the 1850s had a spell (under the name of Hope House) as a co-educational boarding school. The Hatcham Liberal Club acquired the lease in 1885 and remained until the building of the Queen's Road premises, so that it was to Portland House that Bernard Shaw came in 1891 to lecture the club on 'Alternatives to Social Democracy'. The fine old house was demolished in 1914, and soon replaced by the present 228 to 238 New Cross Road, between Troutbeck Road and the Haberdashers' Aske's Girls' School. The school is the vague shape looming in the top left hand corner of the picture.

Of all the fine houses of Morden Hill, formerly Whalebone Passage, once one of the best addresses in Lewisham, the only survivor is Brandon House. It was built in 1845, probably for the ship owner John Lidgett. Like all the properties on the west side of the road, it was eventually absorbed by St. John's hospital. When the rest of the redundant hospital buildings were demolished in the late 1980s, Brandon House was spared, and has been converted into flats.

The Alexandra Hall was built in 1863, at the corner of Bennett Park and Cresswell Park, in the heart of Blackheath Village, and inevitably named after the new Princess of Wales. With its fine meeting or concert room, and its swimming bath in the basement, it served Blackheath well until overtaken by larger competitors. In the 1920s it was adapted for use by Lloyds Bank, and ruined in the process. This postcard shows the hall *c.* 1905.

Lewisham Workhouse and Infirmary, now the hospital, *c.* 1924, when the buildings ranged in date from 1817 to 1894. It has since expanded hugely to the north. Its westward growth has been barred by the Ravensbourne, the sinuous course of which is marked by the belt of trees in the foreground. Beyond the hospital there is a glimpse of Lewisham Park, before any of its big houses had been demolished.

The new Deptford cemetery was established outside the parish boundaries in Lewisham, and soon became known as Brockley Cemetery. It was scheduled to open in 1854, as a replacement for St. Paul's churchyard, but was late, of course, by four years. As the churchyard closed promptly on the planned date, great problems were caused to the people of Deptford until the Home Office was persuaded to re-open it as an emergency measure. This Edwardian view was taken from close to the main cemetery entrance at the corner of Brockley Road and Ivy Lane.

Ladywell Road *c*. 1905 and 1930, showing some of the public buildings that accumulated here from the 1880s. The baths are on the left, and the St. Mary's parish hall (to which the institute had been added by 1930) on the right. The date of the top picture must be 1907 or earlier, for it was in the winter of 1907–8 that the conical roof of the Ladywell Baths tower was removed. The members of the Baths Committee felt that this feature fulfilled 'no useful purpose, and its claims to be of an ornamental character are . . . more than doubtful', so that its repair was not worth the expenditure of 'any considerable sum'. The estimate was £60.

The last meeting of the Lewisham Metropolitan Borough Council on the 24 March 1965, with the mayor, Tom Bradley, presiding. Lewisham was about to merge with Deptford to form the present London Borough. It cannot be said that any of those who were still awake looked cheerful about their future prospects. The standing in silent tribute to the lately dead Lord Morrison of Lambeth (see I 147) cannot have lightened the atmosphere of what was naturally a gloomy event. Similarly mournful rites were being enacted at Deptford Town Hall (and indeed all across London) as the local politicians came to terms with the upheaval government had wished upon them and their communities in pursuit of an imagined administrative convenience. The meeting was held in the council chamber of the old town hall, itself half crumpled for the dustbin of history. The building was demolished in 1968.

Silver trowel in hand, George Livesey, Engineer to the South Metropolitan Gas Company, steps up to lay the first brick of a new retort house at the Bell Green gasworks, in 1879. Livesey later succeeded to the hereditary chairmanship of the company, and was knighted in 1902.

In the late nineteenth century the designers of public baths often tried to make them look like country houses, whereas the modern architect is likely to have a factory in mind. Forest Hill Baths, seen here c. 1910, were the creation of Wilson, Son, and Aldwinckle, who also designed Ladywell Baths. They were opened by Lord Dartmouth in May 1885, a week after Ladywell. Today the factory system has triumphed, and the people of Forest Hill are having to fight hard to save this much loved amenity.

# THE MARKET PLACE

*Lewisham Market and Woolworth & Co. c. 1970. The shop had been established here at 100 to 104 the High Street just before the Great War, but withdrew into the Lewisham Centre in the late 1980s.*

Carlton Lodge, 2 New Cross Road, seen on the left of this picture, was built in the mid 1820s. An early occupant of the large yard behind and of no. 4 next door was George Shillibeer, the man who introduced omnibuses into England. He built them here in the 1830s. Loder Street, seen on the right, was later laid out across the yard. What little survives of it is now called Chesterfield Way. When this photograph was taken *c.* 1925 the premises were owned by Ben Thomas.

The street market at Deptford Broadway (seen here *c.* 1905) was already well established in 1893. 'There are no stalls', it was reported in that year, 'and the number of hand-barrows never exceed twelve, which are used for the sale of haberdashery, plants and ironmongery . . . The shopkeepers consider it to be a nuisance, as the piece of ground has now become a meeting place for idle characters.' The shop on the right was Peppercorn's department store. (See I 131.)

Deptford's Douglas Way street market *c.* 1970, seen from the High Street end above, and looking towards the High Street below. The building in the distance in the bottom picture is the Midland bank at the corner of Giffin Street. All these Douglas Way houses have since been demolished and the street itself has a somewhat tenuous grasp on life.

James Garvey Edwards was a grocer and cheesemonger at 321 Brockley Road (in the parade between Adelaide Avenue and St. Margaret's Road) for about fifteen years from 1890. This photograph shows his shop decorated to celebrate Queen Victoria's Diamond Jubilee in 1897. Under the second 's' of 'sandwiches' stands Edwards' eldest daughter Caroline, and beside her are her brothers Percy and John.

There was great curiosity in Lewisham in 1933 when the Royal Arsenal Co-Operative Society demolished the old department store (formerly Stroud's) that it had used since *c.* 1926. What would replace it? Progress in March 1933 (above) gave little clue, but soon the papers published an artist's impression of the modernistic Tower House, which still dominates the centre of the town. It was opened with a great fanfare in November. The design was by the unsung company architect, S.W. Ackroyd, whose name barely figures in the publicity. The Co-Op was still open in 1960 (below), but Tower House was already beginning a decline towards closure and near dereliction. Last year it was re-opened as a wine bar, things now as common in Lewisham as department stores were seventy years ago.

The homoeopathic chemist William Butcher settled in Blackheath *c.* 1868, and moved his business to 33 Tranquil Vale (seen here) in 1885. This photograph, very likely taken by Butcher himself, can probably be dated to between 1885 and 1895, when the firm became Butcher, Curnow, and Co. They expanded into various other fields, notably photography, and did not finally leave this shop until 1990.

Paragon Place, formerly Paragon Mews, began as a service road for Montpelier Row. Gradually the stables passed into the hands of carriers and jobmasters, who in time gave way to motor engineers. In the 1930s the road was dominated by Newman & Williams, who had three distinct premises. This was their garage at nos. 15 and 16 on the west side (with the garden of Colonnade House behind). It was demolished in the early 1950s to make way for the Ryculf Square estate.

Herbert Baker's grocery and off licence was established at 229 Lee High Road from *c.* 1900 until the early 1930s. This shop, the second from the corner of Dacre Park, sold groceries until quite recently, but is now part of a furniture business. The frontage was altered in 1906–7, when the road was widened during the laying of tramlines.

This Edwardian view of Springbank Road looks towards the corner of Duncrievie Road on the left, and the old entrance to Hither Green station on the right. This was part of the estate created by 'a large speculative builder, Corbett', as he was described in 1899. 'There are two shopping centres on the estate, one in Springbank Road which has a kind of parade called "The Market" at the north end . . . not yet very flourishing.'

The Broadway, Catford Road was built in 1927 by James Watt, the leading local developer, on the front garden of Elmwood, the Catford Conservative Club. The prominence of the new parade soon led to the road behind the town hall having its name changed from Springfield Park Crescent to Catford Broadway. The biggest shop in the Broadway was the drapery store of Edward Jones at nos. 10 and 11. It is seen above in the 1930s, with the manager, Thomas Smith, in the doorway. William Jones Goodrum, the bootmaker, who established himself at 5 Springfield Park Crescent *c.* 1913, would find his address changed to 21 Catford Broadway if he could return today.

The firm of Joshua T. Allder, now known for its department stores in Croydon and Bromley, began in 1877 with a small drapery shop in Rushey Green. The business expanded into adjoining premises, and there was eventually a large furnishing department a few doors to the south. The original group of shops, 100 to 104, was rebuilt in 1928, as seen here. Allder's remained at Catford until the late 1960s. Boot's the chemists then took over the shop, which has since been rebuilt again.

The shops in Bromley Road, between Old Bromley Road and Downham Way, were built by the London County Council as a convenience for the tenants of its 1920s Downham Estate. They are little altered today from their appearance here, when new. (See II 96.)

The Colosseum, at the corner of Dartmouth Road and London Road, was an aspiring Forest Hill department store of the 1890s. The main part of the shop occupied 1 and 3 London Road, formerly 1 and 2 Prospect Villas, a large pair of houses of the late 1840s. The shop soon failed, and the predator lurking on the left of the picture was ready to pounce. This was the London and South Western Bank (now Barclay's) which acquired the site, and rebuilt the corner as it appears today.

# GETTING ABOUT

*The view north along Lewisham High Street from the clock tower to the Obelisk in the 1890s, when the horse tram ruled the road.*

Tranquil Vale was the traditional rank for the cabs that ferried the Blackheath City gents from the station to their homes. In this view from *c.* 1873 the cabs are lined up outside the old Three Tuns (the wooden building with the bay windows), twelve years before its sad rebuilding. The horse cabs did not finally disappear from Blackheath until the 1940s.

Thomas Tilling, the greatest of the horse bus proprietors, was a Lewisham resident, at Perry Hill Farm, and a key figure in the local transport system. This London Bridge to Deptford Broadway bus was photographed *c.* 1900. It was standing outside Haycraft and Son's cycle warehouse at 2 King Street, now Harton Street. This building connected at the back with Haycraft's main ironmongery shop at 46 Deptford Broadway.

The Deptford Wharf Branch, a freight service linking the London & Croydon Railway with the Thames, opened in 1849. It had to cross the Surrey Canal by means of this lifting bridge. Only when the bridge was raised could barges pass along the canal. The photographer who recorded this scene *c.* 1905 was standing outside the Mazawattee tea factory (see p. 18), and looking north-west. The distant building on the right was the signal-box at the Bricklayers' Arms Junction.

The creators of the London and Greenwich Railway (London's first) floated a number of eccentric schemes. One was the creation of wide footways alongside the viaduct at Deptford, which they expected to become 'fashionable promenades'. This fragment, seen in 1911, was in Edward Place, at its junction with Hamilton Street. (See p. 34.)

The London Bridge train picking up its load of commuters from platform 3 of Lewisham Junction station, a scene as familiar today as it was before the Great War. The huge middle-class expansion of Lewisham in the 1850s and '60s was driven by railway development. The process was begun by the opening of Lewisham station in 1849, and accelerated by the addition of the Mid Kent Line in 1857. This necessitated the removal of the station from the High Street to its present position.

The opening of Hither Green station in 1895 was the making or breaking of the suburb. The coincidence of this event with the building of the Park fever hospital, and the decision of the Earl of St. Germains to put his farmland on the market, created the opportunity for large-scale development, and ensured that it would be mainly in the form of lower middle-class housing. This photograph of the station from the Lewisham direction was taken in the late 1890s.

Catford station, on the London, Chatham, and Dover Railway, was opened in 1892. This postcard of *c*. 1910 shows the old booking hall beyond the bridge, in Ravensbourne Park, which has long since been demolished. Its replacement has been built on the site of the lock-up shop on the right of the picture.

There have been three booking halls on the up platform of Forest Hill station. We know little about the first, and all too much about the third. This was the second, which was built between 1880 and 1884 (some way north of the old site), and badly damaged by a flying bomb in June 1944. The ruins were demolished in the 1970s.

This spur from the Deptford Wharf Branch (see p. 95) ran down Grove Street to serve the Foreign Cattle Market and its successors. In this 1930s picture the Victualling Yard wall is on the left, and on the right is the Victoria Tavern, formerly the King's Head. The two cottages beyond the pub were probably built in the 1780s, shortly after this part of Grove Street was created. The Victoria is one of the few old buildings surviving there. (See I 85 for another view of this unusual railway.)

The meeting of the old and new transport systems at the southern end of Rushey Green *c*. 1910. As a Tilling horse bus swings into Catford Road, an electric tram waits to begin its journey towards Greenwich. Rushey Green was the tram terminus until the extensions to Forest Hill in 1913, and to Southend in 1914.

The running of tramlines along Lee High Road in 1906–7 must have been a shock to the residents of that wealthy district. This photograph, taken soon after, shows the gardens of some of the big houses: Lee Place, now supplanted by a huge car showroom, on the left, and Torrington Villas, the site of the Mercator Estate, on the right. Beyond is the now truncated Blessington Road (see p. 123), and the parade of shops running to Lewisham High Street.

A charabanc outing preparing to start from Milton Court Road in the early 1920s. The vehicle was probably parked on the west side, near the corner of Abinger Road West, but it is hard to be sure when so little of the road survives (see p. 121). There was no pub or club nearby to give a clue to the sponsor of this treat.

This bus stop at the junction of New Cross Road and Lewisham Way, opposite the Marquis of Granby, offered a menu of services in 1918 that is surprisingly like the modern one. Behind it is Clifton Hill (now Clifton Rise), with the ornate New Cross Inn on one corner, and the site of the New Cross Kinema (see p. 103) on the other.

# FUN & GAMES

*The saloon bar of the White Hart, New Cross Gate, a pub founded in 1846, but rebuilt later in the century.*
*(For the exterior see I 53.)*

The Marquis of Granby probably had its origins *c.* 1760, when the hero of the Seven Years' War was at the peak of his fame. This 1920s postcard shows it as rebuilt in 1868. Pubs sometimes acquired collections of miscellaneous curios (miniature Horniman's museums) as extra attractions. On the left is the New Cross Wesleyan Church, for the interior of which see p. 51.

This was a routine photograph when taken *c.* 1970, but already it has acquired an historic quality, as the Den sinks deeper into the memory. Millwall FC, which had been founded on the Isle of Dogs in 1885, had its headquarters here in Cold Blow Lane from 1910 until 1993.

The New Cross Kinema, the last and grandest of the borough's silent picture palaces, was opened in 1925. In addition to its vast auditorium, it boasted a dance hall, a cafeteria (see I 127), and a large orchestra. The manager was always looking out for publicity stunts. In 1926 he screened, during the week that included Armistice Day, *Every Mother's Son*, a film 'founded on the theme of The Unknown Warrior', and starring Rex Davis and Jean Jay. The leading lady was brought down to New Cross for a personal appearance. Here the staff, in their brown and gold uniforms (plus a sizeable part of the audience), are seen posing with Miss Jay. Those patrons who were left cold by the patriotic theme need not necessarily have gone home disappointed, for in addition to *Every Mother's Son* the programme included *That Royle Girl*, a 'thrilling melodrama by D.W. Griffith', and a live performance by Bert Bray, 'the Baritone Comedian'.

The Gresham Sports Club in Eltham Road had the ground to the west of the Ravensbourne Club (see p. 116). This postcard view was sent home to Bath in 1905 by a sportsman, presumably a bowler as he chose a picture of the bowling green, who was competing in a championship here. 'We are feeling fit,' he wrote, 'and living in hopes of being the Cup holders in a few hours.' The view is north towards Manor Way. The building in the distance, with the strange turret or gazebo, was probably no. 28, but if so this ornamental feature had disappeared long before the rest of the house was demolished in 1963–4. Owners of the earlier volumes of this series may care to note that the lower photograph on page 114 of *A Second Selection* almost certainly shows the front of the pavilion featured above, which would make the pair of houses in the background of that picture the present 35 Eltham Road. The Gresham pavilion no longer exists, but the area is still devoted to sport.

The retired farmer Charles Edward Bowditch lived at Holly Lodge, Wisteria Road, throughout the sunlit Edwardian decade. Here his children and some of their friends are seen in the depths of the garden, which is now a car park. His eldest daughters were Kate, Elsie, Ethel, and May. (See II 119 and 121.)

The annual jamboree of the Lewisham and District Horse and Pony Show and Parade Society was held off Bromley Road from 1899 to 1904, but was then switched to Horn Park Meadows in Eltham Road, an area now covered by Crathie Road, Scotsdale Road, etc. At the 1907 Lewisham Horse Show most of the prizes were carried off by this fine roan gelding, the property of Walton & Co. of Greenwich.

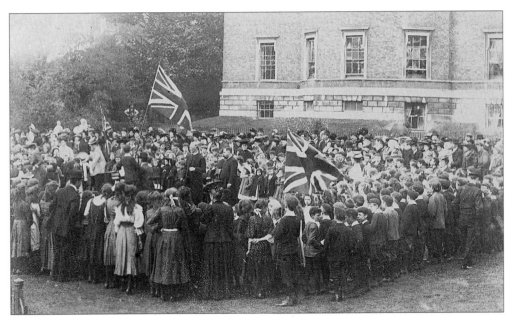

Empire Day, the 24th. of May, was celebrated in all schools with processions, speeches, special history lessons, and the singing of patriotic songs. Apart from the obvious favourites, these might include something more sophisticated, like Kipling's 'Recessional'. Most ceremonies were confined to playgrounds, but in 1907 one school (almost certainly Northbrook) took its piano into the grounds of the Manor House library at Lee.

The South East London (later the Lewisham) Banjo, Mandoline, and Guitar Club posing behind the St. Mary's Schools in Lewisham High Street in the 1930s. The parish church is in the background. The club was founded *c.* 1929, and, extinguished by new fashions, met for the last time in 1954 at the Excelsior Club in Ennersdale Road.

The King's Hall at the north end of Lewisham High Street (see I 125) was one of the most attractive of the borough's cinemas, but its flamboyance was out of tune with post-war austerity, and when the hall was reconstructed after bomb damage it emerged as the dull Rex. In its last decades, the 1970s and '80s, the cinema was twinned as the rather disreputable Studios 6 and 7. *The Magic Christian* and *Far from the Madding Crowd* were shown in March 1970.

The Central Hall at Catford, now (as the ABC) the borough's only cinema, is seen here in 1916. It had opened three years earlier. James Watt, the canny proprietor, kept down costs by letting the upper floors to Clark's College, which specialised in preparing candidates for the Civil Service exams. Its advertising put the cinema's quite in the shade. (See II 72.)

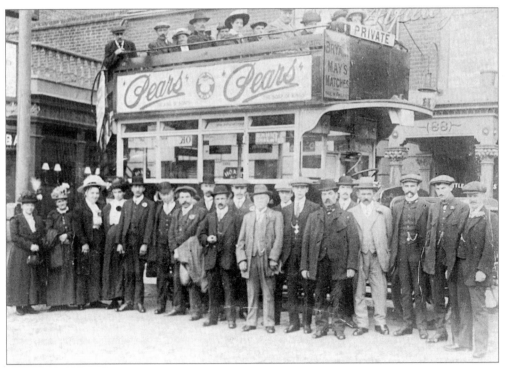

Pub outings were an important feature of working-class social life in the early decades of this century. This one was about to leave the Rising Sun, Rushey Green, *c.* 1910. The pub, which was founded in 1823, was to be rebuilt in 1937. As another symptom of the destructive madness now gripping the brewers of England, it has recently been re-named the Goose and Granite.

The Private Banks Cricket Ground at Catford, still a miraculously preserved expanse of green in the heart of civic Lewisham, opened in 1874. The first groundsman was George Hearne, who had played for Middlesex. He is seen here in 1876, outside the old pavilion. With him are his sons, who went on to play for Kent and England; one played for England and South Africa. (See I 77.)

The 1920s was the heyday of the amateur dramatic societies. In Lewisham there were dozens. The Katagum Players were run by Cyril J.T. Roe of 34 Carholme Road, Forest Hill. He is probably the central figure in the group above, posed in the garden of his house during a break in rehearsals for a drawing room comedy. Below is a whumsical moment from his *A Midsummer Night's Dream*, the only production to feature garden gnomes instead of fairies.

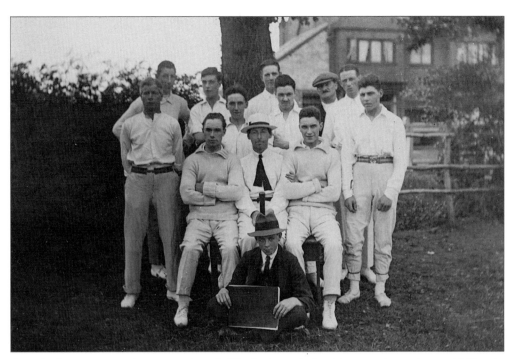

Grove Park was an area rich in sports grounds. The St. Augustine's cricket team is seen here *c.* 1910, at its ground in Marvels Lane, just south of Sydenham Cottages. The buildings behind them were part of the Parade, the shops at the corner of Fairfield (now Luffman) Road. This field is today largely covered by Alice Thompson Close.

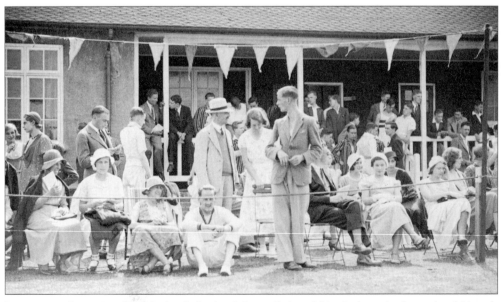

Sports grounds survive along the borderlands of Grove Park and Mottingham, in the angle of Marvels Lane and Grove Park Road. This was the scene in 1932, during a sports day at the City of London College Athletic Ground. The pavilion still stands, but has been greatly altered. The future of this playing field, most recently used by the City of London Polytechnic, is now in doubt.

# GREAT WAR

*Bellingham Road from Bromley Road c. 1917, when the long lines of Army Service Corps vehicles gave it quite a modern appearance.*

The army invaded Blackheath early in the war, driving the golfers from their bunkers. Holly Hedge House, long the headquarters of the local volunteers, was turned into a major recruiting centre, and this traditional parade ground became the frequent scene of reviews and inspections. As air attacks developed the Heath was also used as a location for searchlight units. This formation of horse artillery (seen near Montpelier Row *c.* 1917) was one of many that found rest and refreshment on Blackheath.

West Lodge, seen here *c.* 1918, was built in 1880–1 at the corner of Love Lane (now Heath Lane) and Eliot Vale, on part of the grounds of The Cedars, Belmont Hill. When The Cedars was being used as a military hospital, West Lodge served as the officers' mess. (See I 41 and II 103.)

The Deptford war memorial was erected in Lewisham High Road, now Lewisham Way, in 1921. The designer and builder was William Richards of 333 Brockley Road, and the sculptor W.W. Wagstaff of Kingston. In this early postcard view Upper Brockley Road can be seen to the right of the memorial, and on the left is the Brockley Congregational Church, which was to be demolished in 1968.

Alderman A. Hume Nicholl, the mayor of Lewisham for much of the war, often sported khaki as Lt.-Col. of the Lewisham Cadet Battalion. On 25 October 1918 he opened a sale of work in aid of the comfort fund of the Lewisham Military Hospital (see I 150). With the mayor in this group of dignitaries was Cllr. Harry Chiesman, the department store owner, who remarked, amid laughter, that he always liked sale days.

For the first year of the war the Ennersdale Road barracks served as headquarters for the 2nd/4th London (Howitzer) Brigade, the second line of the Lewisham Gunners. Volunteers poured in and received their basic training under Lt.-Col. Finch, a veteran of the Zulu Wars. The corporal in this picture is seen near the barracks entrance, with Ennersdale Road in the background.

As the Great War dragged on potato shortages became a serious problem for housewives. Long queues (see I 152) became a wearisome feature of everyday life. The example seen above and below ran down Rushey Green and way round the corner into Holbeach Road. The distant goal of all these hopeful purchasers was the greengrocery of George Painter and Son (see II 88), at 86 Rushey Green, next to the Rising Sun.

When thousands of Army Service Corps men descended on Grove Park and district the local churches rallied round to provide comforts and moral support. This was Burnt Ash Road Congregational Church, which had been built in 1876, and was to be destroyed in 1944. The soldier who sent this card to his mother in Aberdeen in 1916 wrote that it was 'a Photo of the Church & Club you address my letters to'.

The Ravensbourne Athletic Club's playing fields in Eltham Road were well established when an ambitious residential club house (seen here in 1916) was added to the facilities in 1913–14. This was just in time for it to be requisitioned, like so many other properties in the area, as an army billet. It returned to its original function after the war, but since the 1950s has been converted into flats as 130 to 184 Eltham Road.

The Greenwich Workhouse, later Grove Park Hospital, served as the Army Service Corps' No. 1A Reserve Mechanical Transport Depot almost throughout the war, and processed many thousands of troops on their way overseas. Blocks G and H were used for the reception of new recruits. Large numbers of them are seen assembled outside in this postcard, most not yet provided with uniforms. (See I 149.)

One of the countless billets used by the Army Service Corps was Holly Bank, 148 Burnt Ash Hill, seen here in 1917. The house, which had been built in the late 1870s, was replaced by the present block of flats in the 1960s.

Woodcroft, no. 263 Baring Road, was built *c.* 1880, as one of the first generation of Grove Park houses. Like so many similar properties it was proving hard to let by 1914, and was promptly taken over as an Army Service Corps billet. The military theme continued, for Woodcroft was demolished *c.* 1937 to provide part of the site for Napier House, the Territorial Army HQ built in 1938.

In 1917 No. 4 Billet of the ASC was Chile House, 333 Baring Road. The soldier who sent this postcard home to Hull told his family: 'Well, here's a view of our "City" residence. We do live! But not a bite of bread in house, what about some buns?' Chile House has been demolished, like nearly all the 1870s and '80s houses of Grove Park.

# FORCES OF DESTRUCTION

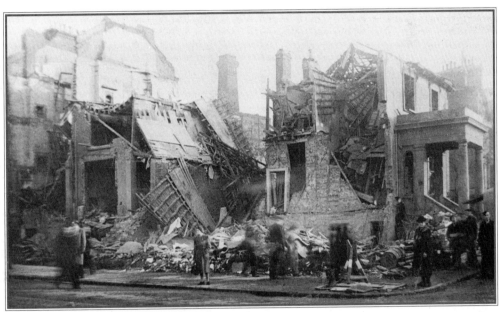

*No. 284 New Cross Road after it had been devastated by the Woolworth's V2. (See p. 120.)*

St. James's, the approach road to St. James's Church, was established in the 1850s. It is seen here from New Cross Road, *c*. 1925. The house with the imposing porch and the eagles (then occupied by a dentist) was numbered 284 New Cross Road, despite having its entrance in St. James's. It was destroyed, as were the houses beyond, by the Woolworth's V2 rocket of November 1944 (see p. 119), and prefabricated council offices, still surviving, were built on the site soon afterwards.

Clifton Hill, now Clifton Rise, seen from the foot of the steep slope *c*. 1914. These 1850s houses were numbers 14 to 70, broken midway by the turning to Walpole Road. In the distance can be seen the taller outline of the Dewdrop Inn. That is, characteristically, the only survivor, because this part of Clifton Hill and the whole of Walpole Road were swept away in the early 1970s to create Fordham Park. Councillor Fordham did more than most local politicians to earn his portion of immortality, for his was one of the houses demolished.

Two studies of old and new Deptford in collision. In the top picture, taken in the 1940s, 40 and 42 Edward Street can see their own coming fate in Sycamore House, the new block of flats next door. The cottages were built *c.* 1780, when this was Loving Edwards Lane. (This was not named after an affectionate Eddie. The developer was Mr Loving Edwards. His unusual first name came from the Loving family, prominent in Deptford in the seventeenth century.) In the 1968 picture below the Victorian houses of Milton Court Road, perhaps the very ones seen on p. 100, are being demolished as the brave future marches down the other side of the street.

The west side of Deptford Green in the 1920s. This is the view north, with the Earl of Romney in the distance. The pub survived long enough to be bombed, but all the houses on its near side (mostly of the eighteenth century) were demolished by the London County Council to make way for the second part of the Hughes Field Estate, built between 1926 and 1936.

This photograph of 112 Lewisham Road was sent as a Christmas greeting in 1910. The house had been built *c.* 1850, and was originally known as 16 Morden Terrace. This Morden Hill end of the row was destroyed during the Second World War, and all was soon swept away. The site of no. 112 would now be between Pitmaston House and the road.

Blessington Road was the key feature of the development that the Merchant Taylors' Company laid out at Lee in the late 1850s. Nos. 16 to 34 were built *c.* 1860, and soon occupied by the solid City men then moving to Lee in droves. The houses survived the Second World War, but when seen here in 1961 were about to lose the peace. Flats called Ericson and Clavering Houses are now on the site.

The building of Avenue Road *c.* 1840 marked the beginning of Lewisham's modern suburban development. Although it was still looking smart when this photograph was taken in 1961, Romer Avenue (as it was then called) was already doomed. For that was the decade in which every ambitious town wanted a covered shopping precinct in its High Street, to ruin the neighbours. A fat planner plonked his big red finger down on the map, and Romer Avenue was dead. Sentence was carried out *c.* 1970, and this is now the main entrance walkway of the Lewisham Centre.

Effingham Road seen from near the Burnt Ash Road end *c.* 1905. These houses on the north side, nos. 6 to 36, were built in the late 1870s. All were demolished in the early 1970s to make way for the Wimborne Close development.

Newstead Road from the Burnt Ash Hill end *c.* 1905. The houses shown here (2, 4, 6, etc.) were built in the mid 1870s. This part of Newstead Road no longer exists. Its destruction was, as so often, the result of a combined operation by the Luftwaffe and Lewisham Council. Kimbolton Close is now on the site.

This is a tale of two roundabouts. Since these photographs were taken in 1969 both scenes have been transformed. The junction of the High Street and Loampit Vale (above) is now the site of the vast northern roundabout of the new Lewisham. Its creation required the demolition of the Duke of Cambridge pub, seen on the right. As the Odeon also came down in 1991, after ten years of closure and decay, only the shops on the left survive to contemplate a radically new enviroment. The photograph below was taken from Limes Grove, and looks across the High Street to Molesworth Street. The southern roundabout now stands here, with an adventure playground rather oddly sited in the middle. All the buildings on the left have been removed to permit the widening of Molesworth Street.

When this photograph was taken from the campanile of the Roman Catholic church, *c*. 1970, the centre of Lewisham was on the verge of a major upheaval. To the survivors of Lewisham 2000 the changes of the early 1970s will be small beer, but at the time they must have seemed momentous. The creation of the Lewisham Centre meant the destruction of the dense network of private houses west of the High Street, the uprooting of many families, and the elevation of Molesworth Street into a major road. On the High Street itself the chief result of these changes was the disappearance of Romer Avenue (on the left of the photograph) and its replacement by the main entrance to the shopping centre. All this has been trivialised by the developments of the last few years, which have included the total or partial pedestrianisation of this part of the High Street, the destruction of many buildings, and the conversion of the rest into theme pubs. The distant hill of Blackheath looks ever more seductive.

# INDEX TO MAIN SUBJECTS